TONI TATI

TONI TATI

TONI TATI

This book is written to provide information and motivation to readers. Its purpose is not to render any type of psychological, legal, or professional advice of any kind. The content is the sole opinion and expression of the author, and not necessarily that of the publisher.

Copyright © 2019 by TONI TATI

All rights reserved. No part of this book may be reproduced, transmitted, or distributed in any form by any means, including, but not limited to, recording, photocopying, or taking screenshots of parts of the book, without prior written permission from the author or the publisher. Brief quotations for noncommercial purposes, such as book reviews, permitted by Fair Use of the U.S. Copyright Law, are allowed without written permissions, as long as such quotations do not cause damage to the book's commercial value. For permissions, write to the publisher, whose address is stated below.

Printed in the United States of America.

ISBN   978-1-949746-79-2   (Paperback)
ISBN   978-1-949746-80-8   (Digital)

Lettra Press books may be ordered through booksellers or by contacting:

Lettra Press LLC
18229 E 52nd Ave.
Denver City, CO 80249
1 303 586 1431 | info@lettrapress.com
www.lettrapress.com

TONI TATI
MAMADOU AGUIBOU DIALLO
ADDRESS: 1694 TOPPING AVENUE, APART N°2
BRONX, NEW YORK 10457

I don't remember the circumstances that led to this. But my mother pushed me and pressed me against her legs. As I fought go get away from that pressure, she made it even more painful. She sat me on her feet and lifted my head. My eyes encountered hers as she leaned to grab my mouth. I could tell her anger from that look. Her headscarf almost fell as she struggled to maintain me.

She inadvertently released her pressure against my frail body as she put back in place her headscarf. I was almost free and running away when she grabbed my arm. I couldn't break away without breaking my arm. Her anger alone could break my bones. So I sat still.

"Today I'll show you how to brush your teeth" She said.

She grabbed a wooden stick and demanded that I opened my mouth.

She knew that I didn't need to open that mouth. She knew that hole. In good weather, she'd ask that I close my mouth in front of people in vain. From outside she's seen the inside of that hole since birth. That hole was open even when I tried as tight as possible closing my lips.

"If you don't open it, I'll do it anyway" she continued saying. I knew she would brush my teeth my mouth closed. She brushed my teeth anyway. She started with that big incisive and went from one end to the other with such intensity and vigor that she had to use all of her strength to maintain me within her legs. But could not maintain me on top of her feet. I slipped and my butt fell on the little stones that were spread throughout the yard. They stung me like bees.

I was bleeding from my mouth. My mother demanded that I spat. It was a bloody mixture of saliva, morve and sweat. I tasted the salt from my tears and the morve from my nose. Their streams went, like rivers to the sea, straight inside that hole. Unless I spat, my mother could not operate inside of my mouth.

She released my head and said:

"Your mouth is rotten!"

"It is smelly"

After demanding that I spit again, she said:

"You are a curse!"

For the first time, I started to wonder.

Two words defined the world for me: like and dislike.

Can it be that my mother doesn't like me?

Was I different is not the kind of question I'd ask myself. Earlier that day, my grandfather was also furious. He claimed that all eyes were on me at the vaccination ceremony that took place from morning to noon. While all kids were there to be vaccinated, I was there to be seen, to make scenes. Not only was I there but showed all sides of my face to the whole gathering which had government officials as well as him, the grand Imam. He said that the most difficult moment for him was when I tried to brush my teeth in public. It was distasteful. It was unbearable. It was a complete disregard for the large congregation. In short I didn't have good manners.

From his front seat, as an honorable guest and host, he saw me put a long stick inside that hole.

For my short memory, it's the first time he dared to talk about my mouth in front of my mother, my grandmother, my step father, nenan ousmaila, Nene baba dyinkan and a few others. It's the first time they talked about me in public. It's the first time they broke their silence about my mouth. I still remember my grandmother's finger on her upper lip. She was thinking while my grandfather was talking about my mouth. What was she thinking about? Me? Her dead son?

His sudden death, years earlier, the same day I was born, only hours apart, always brought tears to her face. She lamented that her son died of overwork and my grandfather was no stranger to his demise and ultimate early death.

My mouth shouldn't be the centre of attention, must she be thinking. She was bitter toward my grandfather. She used to tell me about my father in his makeshift coffin, in his grave, in his deathbed, in his short but thriving life. My presence alone would spark all of these memories.

Now that my grandfather is talking about my mouth, I don't know what would be going on in her mind. Her finger posed on her lip, perhaps her way of concealing my own hole, her eyes open but wandering farther away told me that she was thinking about my misery or my miserable mouth. She was worried. She could not explain to herself or to others why I had such a mouth. Her son as she put it so many times was the sole and only perfect man on earth at that time. Not one single defect! He was perfect in size, shape and in character. She believed in destiny which made it easy for her to accept. But still to her nothing justified my mouth.

Until that fatidic vaccination day, I never asked myself about this mouth. I am not even sure that I was aware of having a mouth, let alone a defective lip. Accusing me of brushing my teeth in public was totally new of my grandfather. My mother was furious. My grandmother, usually simply concerned, became more worried. The danger is not just outside home; it is inside as well which caught my grandmother by surprise. We'll have to fight back. Could I be staying home for the rest of my life? Is it possible to prevent me from leaving home?

From going public with my mouth? How come a grandfather would prevent his orphan grandson from being vaccinated for free? Why an old man would prevent a little child from being cared for? I didn't even know what "behaving in public" meant. I was searching in my little mind, if I had any, what's wrong. I was just myself. I was me. I was also like any of my peers. I wasn't aware of having a mouth, let alone one that nobody wants to see, furthermore one that wasn't admissible in public.

So why this grandfather doesn't like me?

I asked myself this same question the other day. It was another gathering of notables and officials. On his way, he found me. Again in front of people, his following and most of all my buddies, he told me in a threatening voice:

"Are you going?" "Are you ready again?"

"I will not take any more humiliation and dishonor!"

"Keep away from that. Go home now!"

Honor, humiliation were words beyond my comprehension. So why this grandfather disliked me so much?

I went to this gathering anyway. It was more by curiosity than by defiance, more by instinct than by reflection. I followed Sidi, Moudjitaba, cellou, bransori, bakar bhoye longory. I would follow them anywhere, everywhere. Unlike my grandfather, they treated me with kindness. Moudjitaba and sidi call me "mbarin" which meant closest friend. But the rest called me "Toni tati".

This was 1981 as I can tell now. It was the opening ceremony of the very first school in the history of my village. Before 1981, very few knew how to read and write and did so by going three to five miles to thianhe and petel daily and by foot. This new school was built by the village itself and contributions came from as far as France. Every family was required to register its children. But my grandfather didn't think I was clever enough for school. In fact, he thought that I was retarded but didn't have a word for it. One day I was sent to inform him of the passing of an elderly woman, on my way I forgot the name of the deceased. As an Imam, he needed the correct information before spreading the word. This constituted proof of my retardation in his eyes and would cite this memory lapse as an example over and over again. Now for him I am carrying two deadly diseases: a malformation and a retardation.

Here I am. My grandfather sees me in public again. But not brushing my teeth. I still remember myself in line. We were asked to put our small arms on top of each other's shoulder. We formed three queues or more. Around us were women who couldn't sit inside the new school full of men and officials. When I got to the registration table, I identified myself quickly as Mamadaibou. That's how my mother called me. She sounded unique, authentic when she called my name. I still believe she's the only one who knows my real name. It goes deep into my flesh and soul when I hear her utter my name. There is a direct connection between us like the ombilical cord that once linked us. It looked odd to the team that there was no paper on my behalf. No birth certificate or any other piece of identification. My grandfather, once again, was behind this forfeit. Days earlier, Mody Saikou the village chief came home to collect information about kids to be registered for the new school. He was given only Mouctar's birth certificate. Because, said my grandfather, he was everything a family wished for. He was the brightest kid of his generation. He was the most likely to succeed. He would illuminate a room by his warmth, his charm.

My grandmother was an orphan too. Her mother died in childbirth when she was 2 years old. She knew both worlds: illiteracy and orphanhood. She complained about being prevented from reading and writing by Nenan seebe, her stepmother who changed her into a maid a domestic. That in mind, she decided to stop my grandfather. She needed to act quickly and firmly. Their trade mark was to fight each other in silence and in private. Their status called for higher standard. They always agreed in public. An undeclared war was on.

The very next day after that opening ceremony, my grandmother summoned Mody saikou, the chef de village. The discussion went without confrontation. He promised to fix my case. While working on my birth certificate, he told her I could go to school.

When I was beaten by Hamidou kowle on my very first days to school, when he called me "Toni Tati", my grandmother went to his mother and demanded explanation. Their house was right there by the school. I couldn't escape him. My grandmother judged the situation worrisome enough to remedy it. His entire family bowed to her, apologetic. She was, after all, the Imam's first spouse. All of them learnt the Quran in her hands, through my grandfather. They ate there, like all learners of the Quran did. She was the kindest and the most generous of the four spouses of my grandfather. Complete strangers, on the darkest and latest nights could find food and shelter in our home. Hamidou kowle himself had his beginnings of reading and writing the Quran there. His mother said it was a disgrace for them. With profound humility in her voice and attitude, she promised to fix what's wrong in her son. She was a different woman in that little village where everyone is kind of the same. She was of darker skin, heavy but not fat, beautiful with perfect white teeth that contrasted with her dark complexion. She was of Soussou origin.

When Allahi mbemba stole my "production" later that year, my grandmother demanded reparation of holocaust proportion. She was so outraged that she summoned the teacher, the newly recruited teacher, Mr Ousmane, home. For Mr ousmane, new to the village, fresh to his assignment, it was an opportunity to form his network of influence. For my grandmother, it was an occasion to tell him about my story, her worries about me but also her strong desire to see me succeed despite the challenges ahead. She told him also about my father. My father was everything she wanted to see in me. She told him about my mouth too. He kept a very polite demeanor during the entire conversation and empathized more when he heard the story about my mouth. He said several times that he'll keep an eye on me, that I'll be like his own son, that he'll be my mentor throughout his tenure.

Allahi mbemba's family came too, fearing a curse among other things. My grandmother and grandfather were highly regarded, highly respected by his family which was of a different cast and was given land and protection by my great grandparents. Yero, Dian tenen who were his older brothers; Balouta, his mother; Mansata, his sister all would perform manual tasks for them. They would help my grandfather in his farming or cattle herding. They would bring wood from the nearby bushes to both my grandmother and grandfather. They would accompany my grandfather to various ceremonies to carry his various gifts ranging from meat or live goats, sheeps, chickens, even cows to local rice, fonio, corn. Their only salary was his blessings. They apologized profusely for Allahi mbemba's misbehavior.

On my way back from school, one afternoon, I saw a cow grazing in a field near home attended by my grandfather. I learned it was a gift from one of these ceremonies.

Even though I never dealt with a cow of that size before and despite the protestations of my grandmother, my grandfather decided to send me off with that cow to Telire, a faraway place, a valley in the Gaoual region. My maternal oncle, Mody Mamadou Aliou silty, transhumed there when cattle food was to become rare in the dry season in our hilly land. My grandfather spoke to him about the cow and me a couple of days ago. In a secret agreement, I was to join him.

Even though he always treated me as retarded, he said I was smart enough for that long journey with a cow.

When my grandmother reminded him that I would miss school if I go that far, he laughed of a strange laugh. In real life, he almost never laughed. He was so serious and austere that women of all ages would scatter along his way. Except major ceremonies, he would leave home only for the mosque or the cemetery.

He wanted to say something about school or me, probably both me and school. My grandmother posed to listen. He said nothing.

He proceeded to explain the route. Using his finger, he draws lines to the sand. Visibly not understanding nor comprehending geometry, he told me to open my eyes and ears not my mouth.

He told me the route again and ask me if I got it. I said yes, fearing his sarcastic reaction if ever I dared to say no. Intimidated, I couldn't remember a word.

Seeing his fury, my grandmother came to the rescue and proposed that I go with someone who knew the route. "Who?" "Who?" "Who?" asked my grandfather who has decided to send me away despite the odds and feared that I could escape his plan simply if someone else offered to do the job alone. I should never appear in public again. My destiny was the wilderness. Cows would make me a better person, not school "Mody Aliou's twins do this trip all the time. I admire their courage and abnegation." Added my grandfather.

Alsana et Alsainy, the twins in question were younger and smaller than me. I felt humiliated when he continued:

"Their younger brother, despite his one eye, covers that distance in no time."

Amasadio mysteriously lost one eye that was growing bigger and bigger and out of its orbit and made him look like always crying because of the secretions.

I felt like in tears. If in the eyes of my grandfather, despite this cousin's eye, he's worth more than I My grandfather could tell he has hurt my feelings.

I wanted to jump and fly this cow if necessary. My grandfather knew my psychology.

"Mamasalioulory, Aissatoubinani's son could help this naive of ours bring this cow to where you destined it." Proposed my grandmother.

I knew Massallory. He lived a mile from my maternal grandmother's house where I was born. When I came with a different mouth, his mother nenan Aissatou Binani, and a few others, had the privilege (or horror?) to see me first. I was born in their hands. They washed me first. They wrapped me first. They could feel my strong desire to live, they all say. Despite my mouth, I did, to their surprise, what all normal new borns do: I went for my mother's breasts, seeking milk. Despite my mouth, I was able to swallow. I was already a strong man, they say. But, apparently, my grandfather remained to be convinced.

Massallory was born a couple of weeks later. He was black like coal unlike his mother and father, my maternal uncle Mossadoulory. This short cousin was like a little monkey in the nearby bushs. He knew the name of every single plant and tree and corresponding wild fruits. I learned from him what's edible from what's not. The avocado tree behind our mudhouse was from their garden. He gave me the fruit as a gift and taught me the secrets of germination before our science teacher did.

My grandmother sent me to see if, by any chance, he could be home.

His mother didn't put up any resistance. When you are called by the Imam or anyone of his family, for that matter, you have to respond diligently.

Massallory came. My grandfather praised him for his enthusiasm for the mission. He didn't need lengthy instructions nor geography lessons.

We took the cow. My grandfather told him to never let me lead him or the cow. He ordered me to stay behind the cow. Salt mixed with the outlayers of corn skin was ready. This in one hand and the rope in the other, Massallory led me and the cow to our destination.

When we got outside of the village, he instructed me to get a stick. My job was to hit the cow if necessary or to prevent it from going astray. The path was becoming narrower and narrower as we got farther and farther away from inhabited areas. Less and less human footprint, more and more animal ones. It was much longer and harder than said my grandfather. Forests and clear views succeeded each other. Clearly these paths were made not by humans but by animals. Puddles and streams, cliffs and valleys made the journey torturous and longer. Insects, lizards and snakes made me fear for my life. But, as they became more and more frequent, fear was slowly replaced by amazement. I reacted to the colors, sizes, shapes while Massallory seemed undisturbed. He quickly became friend with the cow. It was a female, not unruly at all. As he gave her the salty provision, she followed him like an old couple. I was left to wander my eyes in this wilderness I've never seen before. Back in the village, my grandfather was lost in his mind, wondering who of the cow or me would disappoint him first, betraying his hopes of a big herd of cows.

When we got to Telire, it wasn't the village I thought it was. It was an improvised camping in the middle of the jungle. One bungalow where they kept belongings, milk and its products, hamacs for beds; two smaller versions of a bungalow where they kept goats and sheeps; nearby a good dozen of newly born and younger cows. I was imagining much bigger and spectacular site.

I saw nenan Niara. I recognized her immediately. She used to visit my mother to whom she was related. She was unmistakable. She was schizophrenic and kept the same dress the same way all the time. One white pearl was always hanging from her braided hair to the side of her forefront. One necklace composed of big and old pearls of amber made her look stylish and classic. She was of dark complexion like my mother. Lately, she's busier talking to herself, to imaginary people (or demons?) and animals. But talking to animals wasn't abnormal to me. My mother talked to everyone, humans as animals. Her conversation with some of her chickens was even personal. I still remember one coq who wouldn't forgive my mother for yelling and throwing stones at them. As soon as my mother turned her back, he would come from behind, targeting her ankles with his long beck which infuriated her. For her, this was a matter of ingratitude. After feeding them, these chickens were always expecting more and this particular one was always the last to leave which resulted and justified the use of force to make them comply but not before a big vacarm, a long argument with my mother. That feather ruffling was always a spectacle in our backyard. Nenan Niara was talking to the goats rather than us. Hopefully, Massallory knew the camping like his own hand. Quickly, he found a place for the cow. Nenan Niara changed her mood and came with water for all three of us. Cows are unpredictable. So is the shepherd.

Mody Aliou silty to whom I was supposed to report to wasn't coming back tonight. Cattle was gone missing. Information about them has come to him. He's gone pursuing those leads. Nobody knew when he was gonna come back, said his wife Djido foune. Together, they've been all over the place. Every piece of information they got yielded no result. She had to return back to the camping to avoid further losses. Nenan Niara alone couldn't handle the situation in the camping, she said. She suggested that we go back home assuring us of her commitment in the well-being of my grandfather's cow despite the challenges.

The night was somewhat quiet and cold. We could hear in the distance strange birds, insects and… monkeys. Mosquitoes sung in our ears before biting us. All around the bungalows, luminescent insects were flying like jets on fire. Early morning, after a cup of fresh milk, Massallory and I left…to my grandfather's disappointment. His plan was to find me an occupation in the jungle, far from school. It could've been anything. I could log trees or become a carpenter, a hunter gatherer if cattle herding was too complicated. He wasn't sure I could learn any skill. But he was certain I wasn't made for school. If I wasn't embarrassing him in public with my mouth, at least he could sleep with a good mind.

When we came home, he was asleep in the veranda outside of his house as he did every evening. We did not disturb his nap. We in fact walked quietly past him. I must say even when asleep, my grandfather was intimidating. I've seen even family members avoid areas where he was known to rest.

From his corner, I've seen the poor man gaze, lengthening his neck tenfold like a fishing bird. He wanted to secretly eat, through his eyes, the world around him. But the whole world was trying to escape him.

My grandmother wanted me to engage him, to be there despite his aversion of me. So, she would send me to bring him water, kola, oranges, bananas or nothing at all, just to ask a simple question. A few number of times, she'd ask me to eat the dinner or lunch she prepared with him. He would say I eat fast, I look at the ceiling not the plate, I don't hold the plate with my left hand, I don't wait, don't follow orders, put my fingers everywhere, if I don't scratch him, I scratch myself. He didn't mention my mouth but it was probably disgusting as well. My grandmother kept silent. But she knew he had Parkinson. He was the one who couldn't keep his hands in one place or plate. He would tremble all over the plate. He had also the bad habit of mixing or messing everything like a bad mason with his long fingers.

When he was outside, I was condemned to avoid his arena. Instinctively, like two felines, I avoided his path. My grandmother knew it but hoped for change.

I told my grandmother about the cow and the journey. I hoped secretly that she would tell my grandfather. I didn't want to risk another humiliation by not telling him what he wanted to hear, run out of words, forget my words or being simply incoherent to my embarrassment. I avoided him the next day and the day after.

My grandmother told me to hide. She knew it could bring trouble if he saw me. She suspected my grandfather's plan from the beginning. Since we left, she was praying for my safe return.

It was easy to elude my grandfather. Except for ceremonies, he would venture outside only if the weather was clement, sunny. His bones were old and rheumatic. The oven in the middle of his house was always lit with firewood where he would bare his skinny legs. From outside I could hear his incessant coughing and spitting.

I wasn't really capable of comprehending intentions, let alone plans. In my life, I've never made a conscious plan. So I never suspected my grandfather's intentions. Three days after my return, it was easy to forget him. Life got back to normal. I missed playing soccer, even though I wasn't known as a good player. They say I played like a wild pig. I was so eager to get behind the ball I couldn't wait until the next morning. To prepare my spirit to playing, I had to make sure that my ball was in its place. Frankly I forgot how I got that ball since I nor my mother could afford to buy one. I hid it in a secret location like an agent inside our mud house. I put it between the "skeleton" of the house and the layers of hay. But it was dark that night. I had no torch nor lamp. But I was determined to see my ball. So I went back inside to the spitfire that served as oven. The fire was dormant in a layer of thick ashes. I used my mouth, yet again my bad mouth would say my grandfather, to blow on the fire. It was hard (the air I assembled escaped from the hole of my divided lip). But if I put the effort, I often got good results. My mother often used my mouth to get the fire cooking. The flames went high which made me proud of my mouth. Quickly I lifted one lit wood and headed toward the back door. The wind blew the flame out. I decided to proceed despite the poor visibility, swinging the tip of red charcoal along the way. Step by step I got closer to my secret location.

I coughed and coughed again. Then I smelled smoke. Behind me there was a trail of smoke. Just above my eyes, everything was full of smoke. Something has caught fire. The house is on fire. My mother's house is burning. I almost instinctively run toward the water jar that was always placed behind the back door. In a decisive move, I aimed at the smoky area. For the first time in my life, I've hit my target. As I looked up, some of the water fell right into my face, blinding me for a few moments. When I was able to open my eyes again, the smoke has moved to another part.

I quickly run outside to call for help. After all, I wasn't that irresponsible despite my grandfather's sayings. It was early. People stayed out late in my village. Before I knew it our neighbors were on the roof, getting rid of the hay, throwing it to the ground, isolating the fire.

Madianbournoumou and his father were particularly active, doing most of the job. I was paralyzed in front of the chaos I've created.

When the largest group of onlookers came, the fire was already put out. A good portion of the roof was useless. A pile of "hay" was on the ground.

I was in my state of surprise when my grandfather came from behind. He had an improvised belt made of fabric around his waist to gather his strength. He had his hands behind his back. When he reached to get a hold on me, I woke up. One big blow to the head almost knocked me out. All of the attention was turned on me now. All eyes were on me, the culprit. I put my hands to protect my head because a second blow was coming. I almost fell to the ground but raised up quickly to run away. My grandfather was cruel but he couldn't run. He was shaky like an old wall. The beating was hurting my body. When I got far enough, I touched my head and hands to see if there was blood. I touched my face. Part of it was swollen.

My grandfather was calling me a cow, a useless cow. According to Fulani legends, cows come only after hyenas for their stupidity. The last time my grandfather called me a name was when he was reluctantly initiating me to the Quran. He said my head was little and shaking like a snake's head. It couldn't stay in one place. I couldn't focus. To get me to do that, he would hold my tiny finger to the Arabic letter he wanted me to pronounce correctly. He would hold it so tight the tip of it would become reddish. If he was really exasperated, he would move the reddish tip back and forth against the tablet, that wooden board of torture. He would say my mouth was only good for food and insisted if my mouth was good for food, it should be good for pronunciations too. It was wrong to mispronounce the golden letters of the holy book. misspellings were also banned. Those early difficulties convinced him of my retardation.

After that incident, for my grandfather, that was it: born with a malformation, carrying a retardation, growing up to become mad, a mad cow...I was useless, a complete, total failure. Nothing could save me. Nobody could save me. Even my grandmother who was clinging to a false hope should let go, thought my grandfather. My mother was completely helpless, voiceless between those two fighting elephants. If she said a word, we would both suffer the consequences.

When my grandfather learnt that morning that the cow he sent me off with to my uncle Mody Aliou is gone missing, he became uncontrollably furious. He was shaking more than usual. It wasn't just Parkinson. He was really angry. To calm him down, my grandmother told him it wasn't unusual for cows to try to find their way back "home". When a cow is new to a place, it has to be monitored, helped during that transition. If not it becomes quickly depressed and try to run away, surely back to its previous pastures. Cows are very attached to their "home country". They also have to be accepted by other cows in a new environment.

Skeptical, my grandfather blamed her for my return. He told her openly that I was supposed to stay with his cow. Now the consequences are: his cow is missing and me the other ultimate cow is setting him on fire. What a disgrace! What a failure!

It was scary. Never before he called me a cow. He threatened to send me off again, this time to Mampatin, a rural area of Senegal. There was no use to keep me home. Some of my maternal uncles lived there, raising cattle and doing seasonal agriculture mainly peanut.

That night, after this threat, I didn't come home. My grandfather could come get me in my sleep. He did that to Mouctar when he stole a tool and a broken piece from a broken truck near home. Both my mother and my grandmother went around asking neighbors about my whereabouts. The next morning, I didn't come home, my mother traveled one mile to her mother for information and to spread the word of my disappearance.

Lunchtime, I didn't come home. Panic is the word to describe what's going in my mother's head. Before sunset, she's returned all stones of the village. No sign of Mamadaibou. Dinnertime, I didn't come home. My mother started crying: mamadaibou, my son, my unique son is missing. let's find his body at least, she told the entire village that has gathered. She told them I may have drowned in the rivers or fell down a cliff or a tree or eaten alive by a wild animal. But let's find out. Let's find his skeleton. She was so delirious that people were dispatched in all directions to find a piece of evidence.

Despite my mother's agony, cries, my grandfather didn't come out He was amazed. How could anyone cry my disappearance? My mother was really out of her mind! In his bed he was thinking of the day I was born, the day my father died. He kept my mother, my widowed mother only out of pity. He could have sent her packing with her dull, ugly baby. It wasn't her that he feared. It's the reaction of the community. If by any chance I disappeared, no big deal should have been made out of it. If I passed away, God has taken back what he gave. He has buried many with his own hands. My mother knew him. he's buried two of her own daughters. They both died in his hands. He simply closed their eyes, layed them down, covered with a sheet. One of them had a lung infection. It was painful to watch as she gave away her last breath. He wasn't emotional then. He's not going to be emotional now for a cow like me.

My mother was inconsolable. She's now surrounded by women of all ages. She's on the ground, lifting her arms to the sky in supplication, sweating despite the cold night, tears rolling down her cheeks.

Madianbournoumou found me. He knew my hideout. we used to hunt birds together. He knew every bird's name and trees they like to get food from. Different trees for different birds. He was a lefty. His sling was a powerful weapon. some other times, he used natural glue from trees and insects to catch unsuspecting, greedy birds. When we came back from one of these expeditions, his bag was always full of all kind of birds. My task consisted of depluming them. He would operate inside of them like a skilled surgeon, separating the good from the bad. Only then we would put them directly in contact with the fire after salting them. He would give me the head, the neck and the fatty ass of every grilled bird. He would keep the rest to himself and his younger siblings he called rats. Food was scarce.

His father was a part time bee keeper. He knew these "rats" were hungry. This was his way of feeding them. He was genuinely affectionate to these "little rats".

He was one of the disciples of my grandfather. He was never able to read or write correctly. His tongue and hands would become heavy like mountains as he put it. My grandfather disliked his left hand he associated with demons. It was a constant battle between them. In school he was often behind two to three days. Mouse Ousmane used to beat him for not being on the same page as the rest of the class. He'd copy his lessons almost like podcasting today.

He never called me "Toni tati". To see the inside of my mouth, he'd rather make me laugh by telling me funny stories which he never run out of. Almost like the bag full of birds, he'd take one after the other out of his bag of tales. My favorite one was the newlywed couple where the groom resembled me in many aspects. Through that story I learnt what married couples do at night. In that way, he took away my innocence to make me laugh, he would also make funny faces. The funniest one was the piggy face where he would augment or diminish his ears, eyes, mouth, nose at will.

When my mother saw me, she was too exhausted to make scenes. Two women helped her go to bed. I realized how much I was loved and missed. Despite my mouth, the entire village cared about me. My grandfather was the only absent. He was furious about a missing cow...

My mother didn't just ask for my mouth to be back but my skeleton too. This was the most irritating for my grandfather. Not only I am alive but I am back too. He would exchange me for his cow.

I've seen my mother cry only a few number of times. Of course, she cried when my sisters died. She cried when her last cow died in a cliff accident where her horns came off even before she hit the fatal ground. My mother had that tragedy in mind the day I went missing. The cow too went missing for two days before been found dead. It was easy to undurstand my mother's wariness. She cried, I imagine, the day I was born because my dad died the same day. How to handle life and death in one head in one same day? It was moving. But to see my mother cry my own death, it's the most moving moment of anybody's life, even mine. I am happy to have witnessed that unique moment.

In school, I wasn't doing well. When they ask me what was yesterday's, even today's topic in class, I simply don't know. Mouctar would intervene to make me look even more stupid. I was bigger than him which added to my stupidity. My grandfather would say:

"Go ahead.

"Tell us, Mouctar"

Mouctar, as to humiliate me more, would mimic even the teacher when reciting today or yesterday's lessons. He was capable of memorizing entire paragraphs. He was bright, eloquent. My mouth couldn't pronounce anything clearly as he does. My mind was almost paralyzed by my mouth. I would form words clearly in my mind and my mouth would betray me. I was the subject of permanent comparison and mockery. My mother got upset a number of times. She even beat me occasionally but couldn't do much to improve my elocution nor my comprehension. She, herself, has never set foot in a school.

My grandmother couldn't read nor write but was determined. We shall overcome!

My grandfather was, day after day, reinforced in his early beliefs. He could stop me anytime. As he wasn't convinced I was doing something important, my school was destined to fail anyway, he started to give me small jobs even when I was supposed to be in the classroom.

One afternoon, returning to school for the class of 3 to 5pm, he asked in a dismissive tone that I get him oranges from the orange tree in the middle of our veranda. I took off my shoes and my schoolbag. I was on top of the tree, on one of the very edges when my grandmother heard us. He was loudly instructing me from the ground to pick this orange instead of that one, pointing his fingers, disapproving when I picked the wrong one. My grandmother was inside, ready for a nap. She opened the window which gave right to the veranda. She saw me almost clinging to a small branch, at the very edge:

"Alahadji, are you going to kill this small boy as you killed his father?" asked my grandmother, her hands in her waist. I could see her from the top of the tree.

"What are you insinuating?" Asked my grandfather, in response.

"Do you realize how dangerous it is? Aren't you endangering his welfare by sending him on top of this tree?"

The veranda was stone paved. If I fell, I would break many bones. But I wanted my grandfather to like me. I wanted to please him. I don't know why he likes Mouctar, not me.

I don't know why my grandmother would upset him at this very moment when we could be friends.

With his trembling hands, my grandfather asked:

"Do you want me to climb this tree? Now you want me to use my own hands, my own legs to climb this orange tree?"

I was now back to a better, more comfortable position as I moved from the edge. I was listening to the argument, wondering if I should get down or stay up there.

"This boy is supposed to be in class right now." Said my grandmother.

My grandfather laughed:

"School again! You going to kill me with your school! What did he learn since?"

"All kids are going to school nowadays. Do you think all of them are smart? Do you think all of them will succeed?" Asked my grandmother.

"I know kids. I have never seen one like this." Replied my grandfather.

"Isn't it too early to tell?"

My grandmother wasn't understanding. Retarded kids get worst not better. I was late. From the top of the tree, I was thinking of Mr Ousmane. Anyone late was going to get a beating. The kneeling down against the black board was also humiliating and painful. We all have wounded knees because of that punition.

"If he goes to school, he's probably not going to burn us alive. We have to find something to turn his attention to." Added my grandmother, trying to find more convincing words.

"But I gave him a cow. You don't want me to turn his attention to cows. I knew you would oppose my decision by all means."

"Why a cow?" Asked my grandmother.

"Skills are learned early" Replied my grandfather.

"It's too early for cows. School is more appropriate for his age."

The wind was blowing. I left the branches for a calmer, safer area. I didn't know who, of my grandfather or my grandmother, to obey. Fortunately, they never fought too long, wary of onlookers. It's not the first time they had an argument. When Bapa Cellou was accused of impregnating Issatou Longory, they had another brawl. My grandfather sided with his son. They both denied categorically and rejected the child. The day Issatou brought the new born baby to Bapa Cellou, he, holding a big knife, threatened to kill both the baby and his mother. When my grandfather asked Issatou why she opened her legs, my grandmother couldn't take it anymore. She grabbed the baby and told my grandfather to shut up three times which was bold to tell an Imam, even if he's your husband. My grandmother knew the whole story. When Issatou and Bapa Cellou started their affair, my grandfather knew it and looked the other way while every Friday he was preaching the congregation to stay away from fornication and adultery.

Ashamed, my grandfather left like a defeated Alfa male. My grandfather left again. He was defeated again. Head down, he took refuge in his room. My grandmother demanded that I get down the orange tree. She handed me my shoes and my schoolbag.

In my village, it wasn't usual or inappropriate to ask for favors or services to schoolchildren going to class. On our way to or from school, people expected us to be available for anything from fetching water to transmitting news or information to other parties. But today, my grandmother told me:

"Go straight to school. You are late enough."

To make sure I was in class, she used to ask Moudjitaba. He never missed a day in school. He always went early to avoid Mr Ousmane's beatings and punitions. My grandmother used him as a monitor, a clock, comparing his time of departures and arrivals to mine. Moudjitaba was an orphan like me, raised by his grandmother. I don't think he enjoyed her company. She treated him like a domestic, freeing him only for holidays. He was the worst soccer player when he hid and escaped his grandmother's tight control.

My grandmother, unlike my grandfather, didn't like the idea of smart children or early giftedness. She didn't trust Mouctar. She, often, described him as an impostor. He knew, very early on, how to make himself look good at the expense of others. She never liked the comparison my grandfather made between us.

"Your mother is really spoiling you. You are too soft" Said my grandfather to me. He referred to my grandmother as my mother because of her being too protective of me, I guess. Today again, he has diverted me from school following my grandmother's two-day absence. She's gone to Djinkan where she maintained a vegetable garden. Two of my grandfather's wives lived there too.

All day we've been busy fixing the rectangular barrier of wood that distinguished our huge property, the Imam's reservation. It was the size of many football fields:

"Your "mother" doesn't want you to be strong. I do." My grandfather continued:

"I've been to Algeria. I fought the war there. I know what it takes to be a man. I want you to be a man. Your "mother" is standing in my way."

We were busy erecting columns of wood after digging the appropriate holes. In between columns we'll stick together branches of smaller dimensions or tiny cut trees. The last step would be a horizontal line of wood stitched at every vertical column by "ropes", natural attaches from trees or trees themselves.

It's not the first time I worked with my grandfather in this tenuous process. This last step was always the most stressful. My grandfather was rapidly losing his strength, his muscles suffering of atrophy. He was becoming shakier and shakier. When he needed to stand on one foot, use his second foot and hands to hold and attach, he would almost immediately fall. By then, we were already separated by the ongoing barrier. From my interior or exterior position (we often interchanged) I would see him ejected a few feet, losing his balance. Even though he'd always accuse me of weakness and softness, he would transform my use of force into madness. Yes, we had to work in tandem but I always did what he asked me to do. I have no notion of proportion, he would mumble. But if I was too soft, he'd criticize my weakness. If the rope broke, it was my madness. If the rope is too loose, it's my softness. If I was too slow to remove my hand or my fingers, he'd simply attach them, calling me a lady in the process. The fact that he had Parkinson complicated things a little more. He was never precise, landing the rope or his fingers, his hands, his feet, his entire body into a different place he intended to. I was responsible for every one of his bad moves. Most of all, I suffered the consequences. My whole body would be aching, specially the tip of my fingers: "You are a cow. You never read my intentions, anticipate my moves, comply to my injunctions, comprehend my explanations." said my grandfather when he caught my finger again in between the rope and the multitude of interconnected woods. Fully aware of my imprisonment, he continued in his shaky operation anyway.

"I don't know when you are going to be good at something" he said, looking at my face visibly affected by the pain he inflicted upon me. Unmoved, probably even irritated by my mouth I used to open when in pain or in emotion, he watched me fall trying to remove my trapped hand. Shrugging his shoulders, he proclaimed:

"Do you really need my cane? I can give you my cane! You are the one who need a cane! I can do without one. You look more tired than a centenarian."

The only time he offered me his cane was when we were doing this same routine outside of the village, this time in his other property allocated to the growing of rice and fonio in the bush of Poyewi. It was a ten-year rotation or so. My grandfather and other heads of the village gathered to decide which field to cultivate.

A perimeter of security was needed to prevent cows, goats and sheep's from destroying the new, tiny plants later, birds and monkeys had to be contained by human presence, noise, dummies, various devices and instruments. But no barrier or fence was high enough or thick enough to protect the crop.

My grandfather was outraged that I wouldn't be mad enough to fall off the cliff surrounding us. Behind my back, it was slippery, deadly also. One case of human tragedy. But many cows are known to have perished by slipping and falling, flying hundreds of meters before hitting the rocky ground. Cows are often tempted by the flowery rice in rainy season or attracted to lonely leafy plants or grass, rare in dry season.

My mother's last cow, her horns coming off and hanging from a small tree, still bloody came to my mind when my grandfather asked me to stand on one foot, push hard with my hands to attach ropes around the cut branches to form the perimeter of security. My survival instinct knew (even if I wasn't fully aware of the danger) I didn't have enough room to manoeuver. Despite his intimidations, I couldn't do much. Frustrated, he flew his cane towards me, almost hitting me but, as I said earlier, he always missed his targets these days. He, then said:

"You are no help! I'd rather be alone! Take my cane! Take it and go home!"

My grandfather was old, too shaky for any kind of job. But I was an escape goat for his ineluctable loss of power and strength. Many found him more and more difficult to work with.

When I told my grandmother about this latest incident, this confirmed only what she suspected a long time ago: my grandfather is pushing me to the edges, psychological edges and physical edges hoping desperately and secretly that I would fall to my own death. Then he would attribute my death to my attention deficit disorder.

Whether it's the edge of an orange tree, the edge of a cliff, the edge of a cracked rope, the edge of his lips, it didn't matter. My grandmother was convinced that my mouth had something to do with his "acharnement", his fury. She thought my mouth put a shame on him even though he would never admit it. For my grandmother, instead of blame or shame, the family should now focus on fixing up my lip.

But Mody saikou, the village chief, came again. It wasn't always good news to have him in your backyard. In the past, he came with armed militia to collect or inspect "duties", taxes very often in nature. Every year, every farmer has to contribute, to give a certain percentage of his crop and cattle to local, regional and state authorities. It went from pepper to cows. It was highly controversial and uneven. Unfairness was the main characteristic of these practices. Conflicts arouse often. Militias used clubs to subdue unhappy subjects. People were injured, jailed or even killed. Many fled the country to neighboring Senegal, Cote-d'ivoire. The village chief was the instrument of the government engaged in a desperate centralized economy. He knew everyone's secrets and alleged intentions. Troublemakers were blacklisted. There were talk of "fifth column". Mody Saikou was ruthless. He didn't like my family he accused of stealing the Imamhood. His family used to hold both the religious and the administrative authorities. In fact, his father was the Imam until he died. He was bitter about his family losing the Imam seat to my grandfather. It wasn't unusual for people and families to kill each other for the altar.

The only time he was nice to us was when he spoke to my grandmother about my birth certificate in a conciliatory tone. This time, when he came, he avoided both my grandmother and my grandfather. He went directly to my mother's house. It was so unusual that my mother thought of hiding herself to avoid him. Many women, in the past, resorted to hiding when they didn't have the pounds of pepper required by the communist regime. Despite her apprehension, my mother came to meet him:

"According to our Intelligence, your son is involved, implicated in the looting and destruction of government property, namely a bulldozer stationed right outside here, in the Longory area."

"Where exactly?" Dared to ask my mother.

"Right by the hill, near Dalanda thianghe's property."

My mother believed anyone who accused me of wrongdoing. Very quickly she concluded I was guilty in her mind. She was lost in her thoughts when he added:

"It is urgent that your son among many others respond to our invitation. I am sent here by the judiciary to inform each family incriminated to bring in their son. Failure to do that will result in the imprisonment and fining of the parents. Those found responsible will have to pay for their actions.

I advise and argue you to commit to the truth and send in your son. it's for inquiry purposes. The committee will determine his level of involvement. This committee is the only habilitated to free him of any wrongdoing. I am in pain. But I have to do this. Either I go to jail or these kids go to jail. I prefer the latter if there is fault." My mother was innately scared of any kind of authority, big or small: her in-law's authority, her husband's authority, the clinical authority, the local authority, the central authority...She was particularly afraid of people in uniform, even medical staff. The idea of dealing with police or militia was simply unbearable.

The most frightening was the idea of me and my mouth sitting in jail, dealing with prisoners and prison guards. Both of those don't like ugly people.

Overwhelmed, my mother has stopped cooking when I came home. She was near the spitfire (oven) but crying. I could see two big tears streaming down her cheeks:

"Did you touch with your own hands the tractor?" She asked.

"What tractor?" I questioned.

For her, anything that's not a car or a truck is a tractor since my grandfather and my step dad brought a tractor for the property's extension and renovation.

"The big thing near nan Dalanda thianhe's house, by that hill."

"Where?" I asked again just to look innocent.

"Longory." After pointing her finger, she dried her tears with it. As soon as I saw her finger, I knew what was done there is discovered now.

A bulldozer was a curiosity, a big curiosity in the village. Many haven't seen one before. Even normal, used trucks are an attraction. kids, mainly boys, follow them all around, all day. Those occasions, we run on empty stomachs eating dust and fumes.

The bulldozer came to rebuild the old road, muddy in rainy season, dusty in dry season. It was never maintained since its conception. Villagers don't use roads. They have quick paths in the jungle to go from one village to the other. That road was the unique link between petel and the neighboring villages. Petel is the center where the weekly market was located. It took place every Saturday. The jail was there too. Everyone knew where the jail is. It was the busiest place during the communist years. If a dignitary of the regime came, he was applauded on top of the hill by people in queues, all wearing the same outfit in the effigy of the ruler. I told my mother I wasn't near the bulldozer. How could that be? She asked. All kids are known to have been there. It was almost impossible for me to miss such an event, the event of the year, a bulldozer in the village, a big, yellow bulldozer in my backyard. The one that built the first road happened when I wasn't born. I could still see its remains. The terrain was so difficult it broke the engine and the body. Its steel wheels remained in place like a dead dinosaur's skeleton, still intact like nature in its purest form and technology in its hardest invention.

She asked where I've been, what I've done, since the bulldozer came. I couldn't remember all of the places I've visited since this strange machine came. In a day, we could go from playing innocent games to fighting, to looting or stealing whatever the season provided and put in our path.

She knew me. I didn't sound believable, truthful. She told me to go immediately see Mody Saikou and explain my version of the events. Naively, she believed he would let me off the hook.

I didn't want my mother to go to jail. It was a serious possibility. At least, I believed it then. So I run quickly to the chief's home which served also as his main office. He was in his living room when I got there. It was probably the first time I entered his house. For some reason, we almost never went there. It was unfriendly probably. Imrana was there but his mother almost never let him play with us. They simply were not our kind.

It was a big house and well furnished with curtains, chairs, tables, artificial flowers, sofas, paintings and sculptures. The verandah was decorated with buckets of flowers and well maintained trees. He had a good taste compared to my grandfather to whom mecca was the only acceptable representation in his walls. In his austere properties, absolutely no paintings nor sculptures. Mody saikou's home was also neat, tidy and organized. My grandfather's houses were littered with old rugs, tanned animal skins, old Quranic books, traditional pencils and ink. In all, he had only one armchair where he napped before it broke. But my grandfather's homes were holier. It looked like simplicity and modesty, even a little disorganization didn't hurt holiness or sainthood. People took off their shoes before entering that small holy land. I didn't take off my shoes to enter the chief's house. Nobody was required to. When he saw me, he immediately took me aside to the lobby and asked me to whisper to his ears my concerns. Much taller than I, he lowered his body, his ears to my bad mouth. I felt privileged. But it was a strategy more than affection or attention. He didn't want people to know, even his own family. He didn't want to face my grandmother nor my grandfather. It was easier for him to deal with my mother and me. After listening with a little sinic smile in his face, he congratulated me for my courage and told me to go directly to the jailhouse where the deputy prefet was awaiting my arrival. A group of ten or more was ahead of me. He told me about them. They were marching fast. I tried hard to catch them. The Idea and the hope of being exonerated and freed were haunting us all and causing us to haste our pace. In the waiting room, we were guarded by militiamen in uniform. One by one, one of them took us in. When my turn came, I declined my identity and quickly told the deputy prefet:

"I didn't cut any wire. The bulldozer was littered with cut wires when I got there. I may have taken one or two but not the entire stuff."

The deputy prefet took note and I was escorted to my cell. It was a vast room. There, I found Sidi, Saikou Yaya, Saiba, Massal Misside, Madian Horelelou, Cellou Horelelou, Bransori, Brandjogo, Jacob. Mouctar and Bakarbhoye Longory joined us next.

It felt a little bit strange. At first, we didn't fully understand why we were sent here. When leaving the "courtroom", we all thought, we were being escorted home.

The cell was the size of a regular room. It served other purposes rather than hold inmates, probably. Most likely, we were too small for an individual cell.

On the bare, cold floor, we sat. When the night came, we were still hoping for signs of freedom. They disappeared in the darkness of the night. When the doors closed behind us and we heard the boots of the guard in the distance, we realized we were about to spend our first night in prison. We didn't eat but it never felt lonely. We even have the luxury to swing few jokes about each other before being swept away, one after the other, by a deep sleep.

The morning came quickly. We were all hungry and eager to go to the bathroom. We, for the 1st time, realized the price of freedom and the horrors of imprisonment. We couldn't eat nor could we go to the bathroom.

When it became clear, around noon, that this bulldozer matter is serious, the weakest of us started to cry. Bransori and Bakarbhoye Longory were first. They complained about headaches and stomach aches. Help never came. The guard who responded to the cries asked:

"Do you think you are in your mother's house? Or you think probably I am your dad!?"

By sunset, we all have come to the conclusion that crying in a jail cell is a failed strategy.

We could not hold our urine any longer. In the darkness of our cell, we smelled a mix of urine and feces. When daylight came, the room was almost unrecognizable: feces and urine everywhere. Inmate visitors and guards held their noses. Our cell room was very close to the main prison entry. Flies were entering and leaving it like a beehive

That second morning, we were given permission to use the guard's bathroom located right outside, on the right corner of the prison building. It was a summary, primitive bathroom: a hole, two or three stones surrounded by old, empty, cut bags of rice put or tailored together for the comfort and subtraction of the guards from outside viewers. We will be escorted to that stinky hole for the rest of our sentence.

We were given, each, a banana for breakfast. We interpreted this as a sign of friendship and started to talk to the guards. They, in return, let us play. Armed with elastic rubber bands, we played at shooting at the numerous burdensome flies.

The third night, they gave us a "plastic canvas" to soften and protect us from the cold, stingy, stinky floor. But at night, we used it to partially cover our small bodies against the cold.

I don't know what my mother and my grandmother were doing. For some time, I expected to see them. They may have been intimidated by the Idea of prison. Prison has bad connotations.

What was thinking my grandfather? He was the only capable of preventing any of this from happening. As an Imam, he was more powerful than Mody Saikou. His words weighed more everywhere, anywhere. Mouctar, Bransori and me were his grandsons. None of Mody Saikous' family and clan was among the imprisoned. None of this was fair and impartial. But my grandfather was happy, I presumed. He always wished someone other than him would teach us a hard lesson. He always felt that nowadays kids were spoiled. Even Mouctar deserved a good correction. My going to jail was naturally logical. He predicted that my troubles were just beginning. More was to come.

Mouctar and Bransori were in prison because of my deficiencies, at least my imprudence. I certainly led them to this bulldozer. In their known rivalry, I was giving Mody Saikou reasons and opportunities to humiliate and dishonor him.

The fourth day, we looked tired and filthy. We were used to being muddy and dusty. We showered very occasionally back in the village. But the atmosphere in the prison, of being in prison made us look miserable. Before we were happy like piglets in filthy puddles. The lack of shower made us stink, our clothing, already low in quality, started to give away under the heavy dirt. Our unprotected skins started to crack under the weather conditions. Our filthy hairs made us look like mad men. The sixth day, two of Saiba's sisters came with food that reminded us of our village.

It was Saturday, day of the weekly fair market. For the first time we ate really good food.

Our grievances heard. Saiba vomited just to get his sisters to tell his mother he was in really bad shape. After that, we started to receive regular visits. Our mothers organized. Each inmate family got a day to bring in food. But my mother nor my grandmother came. Mouctar's mother came on behalf of our family.

On the fifteenth day, nothing was entertaining anymore. We were asking for the bathroom all day just to feel a little room and freedom like fishes gasping for air. Shooting flies and mosquitoes in midair or on the floor was no longer funny, has even become a boring game. We were tired of each other, tired of being kept like slaughter animals in cages. Massalmisside got furious when we joked about his runny nose.

Back in the village, the affair of our imprisonment has become toxic. The village was more divided than when Mody Saikou, always him, and Alhadji Babagalle, another aspiring Imam, decided of the lashing and bashing of our big brothers for partying with girls in one of the classrooms of our school. The village has never been as divided. Mody

Saikou, Alhadji Babagalle, Allahi Bererou and their supporters were the hardliners. They wanted more restrictive laws and broken window policies. My grandfather was also a partisan of punishment but he felt targeted and marginalized. The next Friday, he called upon his congregation to end the suffering and the division. He called upon good Samaritans to help in the effort to collect funds to fix the damaged bulldozer.

Soon after that call, we were freed. Without any kind of protocol, we left the prison like freed birds after long months of captivity. In small groups, we went, each, according to the part of the village we inhabited. Each part has its shortcuts. Sidi, Saiba, Bakarbhoye Longory, Bransori, Mouctar and me lived west and relatively close to each other. To avoid bad luck again, Saiba advised us to find our own way home, to avoid known and frequented paths. In his wisdom, he said it was particularly bad for a prisoner coming home to meet other people on his way. Even without any path whatsoever, we knew how to go.

We took to the bush. Midway, we took a shower in the Doubalya river. Saiba said, still in his position of Wiseman, it was particularly bad to bring prison dirt, prison scent, prison smell, prison odor, prison dust in our homes. He said, we need to feel like new, reborn again. We even laundered our shirts, our shorts to wash away our unfortunes.

My mother and my grandmother never asked. We never talked about this episode of our lives.

My grandfather said my mouth was responsible in the imprisonment of Mouctar by giving a false lead. He said I was ridiculing him in public.

My grandmother said if everyone was accusing me of wrongdoing, it was because of my mouth. My mouth was attracting too much talk. Even my mother said I was famous like a fox in a chicken farm. Everyone has me in their tongue. She told me this when shaving my prison hair. It wasn't just about me, Mamadaibou. They, all, had my mouth in their tongues.

My grandfather decided to give up on me for good. Prison, for him, was the work of evil. Prison is one of the devil's houses. The other house is the dancing clubs. He said: "take your son. Lawbreakers are not of my blood."

From there on, I had two mothers. My grandmother surpassing my mother in care and attention. She started to examine my mouth meticulously, thanking the lord profusely for having created and placed a big incisive inside to protect and hide "me" from the outside world. For her, it was a consolation and a sign that the lord cared about me. She examined me again even lifting my chin to observe and see better. She concluded that my organs weren't in bad shape as she feared. I let her touch me again. It was the first time someone was touching me there a soft touch. It felt good. She tried to reconnect one end of my lip with the other. She did it again and again. She sighed and said her dead son was in me. I looked like her son but disfigured. She looked inside of my nose like an experienced doctor. That's when she decided of my operation. She said she'll put all of her energy and money into my lip or what is left of it. If necessary, she'll sell her last cow, her last ounce of gold and silver to cover the cost. But first, she's going to talk to her sons: Mamadalpha, Addouramani, Ibrahimabano, Mouttapha. She's even going to ask her only surviving daughter to assist in this project of beautification of my face. Aissatou has been always on her side. In general, all of her children are very supportive of her, thank be to the Lord. It's never easy to raise her own family in addition to guests talibes and kids from the neighborhood and those of her co-spouses. Today, praise due to the Lord, she's tending only to the poor and sick.

Mamadalpha is the one she counted on the most. She was proud of him. In the past, she was mainly proud of her cows and vegetable garden. Then came her sons. When their number went from one to five, she stopped counting on her cows and garden. When her husband became Imam, she started to tell her growing followers about her past life as an orphan deprived of any kind of education, about the mud house where she raised all of her twelve children.

Today, she's proud of her spacious brick house, its five rooms. But her last acquisitions: a solar lamp and a gold colored watch that blasted mecca a'zan each prayer time were her favorite belongings. Going to mecca was her most precious tale. Mamadalpha gave her all of that. Since he came back from America, he's the talk of the town. He has achieved what nobody has in the history of the village. My grandmother saw this as the ultimate blessing from the Lord for her patience. Every time she talked about her son whom she associated with America, the memory of her entire life seethed through. She would go from the time she was in the hands of Nenan Sebe, her guardian after her mother died, to the time she held her returning son in her hands.

I've never heard of America before. School didn't teach us geography yet. My grandmother never forgot a word her son told her about America (maybe for having not wasted her brain a classroom, her memory was almost virgin.

Whatever she heard, she kept like a tape). It was, in a way, my first trip, through my imagination, to that land. My grand never had, or even heard of, a map in her life nor did I. I am not sure we had the same map in our heads. But, what her son told her made her even prouder beyond the curiosities, the attractions, the numerous entertainments, the prowesses: America is a country where one loses himself and his identity. Her son fought to preserve his. He told her how he managed to stay himself, stay away from alcohol and women, stay away from drug and crime. He told her it was a country where people chose money over life. They chose dollar bills over values. Back home, back here, we chose values and humanity and community. Which values over which values was the main concern.

He didn't tell her about faith. But she soon realized by herself that it's also a country where one chose to be a believer or not. The thing she was the happiest about was the fact that he prayed five times a day. Freedom of faith was rather a strange notion for her who has lived all of her life in this cage of semis theocratic region, at least former theocracy.

I was more interested in the snow part of the story than the one about identity loss or theft. What is snow? What caused them to have it? How different is it from our fog?

I was forming my own answers because she couldn't tell. We were two worlds apart: she was in the intangible one, I was in the tangible.

Her son didn't become a surgeon in America to help fix my lip. But he has now a job where he earned enough money to afford such surgery. If only his wife let him. My grandmother was worried about her spending spree. She knows. She's been to Lome where he worked as a UN employee.

They didn't tell me until the night before. Neither did they tell my mother. She was never consulted about anything, from trivial things to the life or death of her own children. My grandmother came and told my mother to pack my belongings. That's when she realized it was happening. Finally, Mamadaibou is going to get a new mouth. It hit me too. I became really aware of my mouth. I started to ask myself what's really wrong with my mouth? What is beauty? Why can't I keep my current mouth? Why do I have to be beautiful in the eye of the other? As far as I am concerned, I eat and drink correctly with my mouth, I speak clearly with my mouth. Why do they call me "Toni tati"? why was I born like this? What happened?

I remembered the first time I saw my mouth. It was in a puddle near home after a rainy morning. The water reflected my face but it was distorted. The image was moving as the water moved. I was upside down and seemed much bigger in the water. Mysteriously, the puddle got calmer from time to time. I took advantage of those moments to stare at my face. I touched my lip to make sure it was mine. I made a scene of my face to confirm it was mine. I tried to reconnect the two ends of my lip, in vain. For one moment, I thought of glue to stick them together. Yes, it's me Mamadaibou.

Is this the reason why they called me "Toni tati"?

I decided to really make sure that the mouth I saw in the puddle was mine beyond any doubt. It was troubling but the water could have betrayed me.

The next day, my mother was absent from home. It's Saturday. I saw her take the unique mirror in our house, apply some mysterious powder and sweet lotion in her face. I watched her put on some jewelry and put back the mirror in a utensil. The trend was to put all of your best, newest utensils on a table. It served as a decoration and a display of wealth and fashion.

The table was covered with a square piece of fabric or plastic.

I watched my mother, a bucket in one hand and a purse in the other, go to Petel where the market fair took place once a week. When she put her purse inside the bucket, I knew she's not going to come back pretending to have forgotten her money, if she had any. On the tip of my toes, I went to the table. It was the unique table my mother ever had. It's been there before I was born. It was the table of my childhood. I knew it like a friend. It stopped being intimidating only when I climbed it for the first time. It seemed like the highest mountain on the planet.

Now, I don't need to escalade nor a ladder I chose the right angle to reach and lift the lid of the utensil. The mirror was buried a little bit deeper in a myriad of earrings, needles, necklaces, pearls, gris-gris, "fills" ...

To grab it, I stood on the tip of my toes again. My mother kept it there for safety reasons. Not necessarily our own safety. She wanted to keep that precious object from breaking apart.

I started immediately to examine myself. It was a little bit dark inside. I opened the window which was just above the table. I wasn't satisfied with the result I got neither. The sunlight was too dim. I was determined to see my face before sunset. Not a day more in doubt! I run outside and stood by the main entry. There, I stared at my physical self. Like a professional photograph, I took closer pictures, farther pictures, profile pictures, facial pictures. I held the mirror up, down, close, far. None of these positions made me proud of my face. I was far from satisfied. I was kind of ashamed. I wondered if mirrors too lied like ponds, puddles. What is this? What is this tooth, this bigger than usual tooth in the middle of my divided lip? What is this nose? Why does it look like falling into the gap of my lip? Inside my mouth? My face couldn't express all of my feelings. There was a kind of disconnect, a lack of coordination, a discontinuity. It was bizarre. My face was like a half mask. When my lip stopped in its normal development, it also cut into pieces my emotional self. The waves of joy, fear...couldn't reach all of my face. When I smiled, part of my face was not following like sea waves stopped by an island.

That was the moment I became aware of myself. I didn't cry but I started to know why they were calling me "Toni tati". I took the mirror back. I played as usual but day after day, these pictures grew bigger and bigger into my mind. People were pretending, I was pretending. My grandmother knew it and didn't want to pretend.

She wanted to end the staring and the blaming.

My mother put all of my belongings in a plastic bag. In my life, I never had enough. I never had two pairs of shoes. They bought me shoes and clothing only if the ones I had on all day, all the time, are completely out of order. My grandmother came early, just after the morning prayer. She was telling her beads. She told my mother that my step dad was waiting on me. Now that I was going for real for this big operation, my mother started to panic, to wonder if we'll see each other again. Am I going to be safe? How painful will it be? How much suffering? For how long? Is it worth it?

"They are going to gnassidine." Said my grandmother. The name stuck to my head even though it's the first time I heard it.

I don't know what was thinking my grandfather. Nothing could have been done without his blessing. But, when it comes to my mouth, my grandmother was wary of him. She never trusted him as sympathetic to my suffering. He did not oppose it but he may have thought of it as a waste of resources. What would come out of me? A mouth change cannot change me. We are created perfect or imperfect. The family needed to accept the Lord's order even if he, himself, did not accept me. He found it difficult to accept and accept me.

This departure was significant enough for my grandmother to demand that I say goodbye to my grandfather. I kneeled in front of him to shake his hands. This was probably the first time we shake our hands.

He kept my tiny hands in his shaky but still strong ones for a very long time. It lasted long enough for me to feel some kind of connection, blood connection, spiritual and even mental connection with my grandfather. He was reciting some verses. His lips were moving. I felt loved and appreciated by him. I felt also some belonging to him. When I left to join my step dad who was waiting along my mother and my grandmother, I felt strong. I felt even good.

Ignace Deen hospital didn't look like the shanty town in which it was "deposited". It was like an imported object. Every piece of it looked foreign to my eyes. From the roof to the foundation, to its conception.

Doctors took samples of blood from my step dad who was also my uncle and me.

I've never seen a Chinese before but as soon as I saw one, I made the connection, the resemblance between them and my little sister, Aissatou, nicknamed "chinois" because of her small eyes, her yellowish complexion and her body type.

At first, between the surgeon and his interpret, I didn't know who was going to take care of my lip. They, both wore white uniforms and seemed to consult each other. But when the Chinese, for a preliminary examination, asked me to lay down on a bed in their office, I knew by his scalpel, the seriousness of his look, he's the one who's going to make me beautiful or uglier for the rest of my life. He hit my incisive, with what looked like a small hammer, hard enough to feel terrorized. He returned one half of my lip to examine it inside out. He did the same for the other half. He put his finger, then his scalpel, I guess, to feel, to detect anomalies in the muscles and nervous system. He told me to move my mouth left, then right, my chin up and down. He told me to tighten my lip, to open my mouth, to utter ha ha ha. He examined the inside of my nose with a small torch, lifted it up from its falling position, pushed it left and right to make sure of its solidity or probably feared it would stay in his hands once the operation started.

I didn't feel empathy in any of this. These hands were not my grandmother's nor my mother's. They felt colder under my skin. They were not antipathy neither. These were the hands of a surgeon. He and his translator took notes and measured the area of reconstruction like careful architects, restaurateurs.

When we came back a week later, they told my step dad the blood results were not in yet.

I don't know where he spent his nights but, my step dad came every morning to check on me in this distant relative house where I ate and slept in a cloud of mosquitoes. It was a house where his wife nor his children engaged me. They were condescending. People in cities dislike ugly and unusual people from the countryside. Plus, they were uneased with my mouth. Here, the slightest difference, malformation, deformity could cost you a place in society, could ruin your social life. For the first time, in that house, I felt lonely and rejected. One morning, I was so lonely that I decided to follow Dr Thierno Tallatou Thianghe (was the name of our host) to his office. He was embarrassed. His wife and daughters caught me behind. With their fingers in my mouth and in my forefront, they warned me of serious consequences if I followed him again. This reminded me of my encounter, in Labe, with my uncle Mamadalpha's sister in law where we spent the night en route to Ignace Deen hospital. Mohammed, her nephew was going to get shoes and other gifts from the nearby market. When she saw me behind her, she immediately turned me away with such disgust that I started to form bad ideas about people and society.

The second week, the blood results came in and I was scheduled for the next available date.

Food seemed scarce in Conakry. My step dad and I were both hungry. We were also tired of sleep deprivations because of mosquitoes and other discomforts. They left the lightbulb in the living room on all night long.

I was offered a bed in the hospital a couple of days before the operation. Tasteless food was available and free of charge. The same female and male nurses came every morning to distribute coffee and bread that tasted like waste. In the afternoon, they came again with buckets of rice. Sick of our sickness or tired of the same food, most of it was thrown away to the delight of hundreds of cats that were breeding and populating the area hospital. My room was full of cut and wounded people. One man opposite me was cut and bandaged near the genital area. I watched female nurses touch him there, lifting his gown. Underneath, he had no pant nor slip. I felt outraged and humiliated myself. But, when I found myself defecating in front of other women and men, outside of the hospital, by the Atlantic Ocean, I realized, for the first time, what was dignity and honor to my grandfather's credit. In my traditional village, back home, nakedness was still very much taboo, at least in the genital area. Conakry was starting to decay and collapse under new norms of promiscuity.

Before they got me naked, put in a gown and laid down on a gurney, a man came from nowhere to play the "red nose". From the vestibule that led to the operation room, I could hear the sound of surgical instruments being prepared. Like an animal in the slaughter house, I was frightened. This clown saw it in my eyes. My "dad" was also anxious but didn't want to show his emotions. He was barely talking, just waiting to see me pushed away, to say good bye by his eyes or by his mouth. The man from nowhere resembled the interpret of the other day but his white cap on his head and the surreality of the place made his identity uncertain in my head. My "dad" let him do the talking:

"Don't be afraid. I know you are a strong man." Said the man.

"Tell me the truth. Have you been in love? Do you like girls? Come on." He continued.

I looked at my "dad". I never had such conversation nor a date before. My head down indicated to him that I was feeling uneasy.

"Come on. Don't be shy. We are between us. We're all men here."

His resolve to get into my private life, to get me to tell him my secrets got even bigger:

"Tell me about the girl you have kissed."

Even if I had one, I wouldn't tell him in front of my "dad". He must have known that. But I never had a girl.

I wished I had one.

"You see. Today is the day no girl will resist you. You can date them all."

"Oh, I see, you want to get married and have babies."

He turned to my "dad" for an answer:

"Right?" He asked.

My "dad" nodded, adding:

"That's why we brought him here."

"Do you have friends? The man asked.

I said for the first time:

"Yes." Sidi and Moudjitaba, my "mbarins" came to my mind.

"Listen. You going to have the most beautiful woman of them all."

His hand on my shoulder, he looked like the closest friend I ever had.

For a moment, I forgot what my month's going to go through. A thick door in the operating room opened heavily and a mouth masked man signaled the end of all conversations. When they were strapping my arms unto the gurney, I saw my "dad" disappear, a plastic bag in his hands where he has previously put my clothing. He didn't look back. I didn't see him look back. Probably he did. I was already preoccupied, in my head, with my hands tied up by total strangers. He wasn't more in control than I was in this situation. He may have felt guilty of leaving me behind. But my mouth commanded, demanded such sacrifices. I thought if I want to get married, I'd rather follow these cold hearted surgeons in this room where I heard knives, scissors, scalpels, needles, even hammers call for fresh blood.

A needle placed in my arm reminded me of the vaccination campaign and my grandfather talking about my mouth for the first time. This is probably the third time I was being stung by a doctor's needle. When they pushed me in, I was aware of my surroundings but every muscle in my body was softening, weakening. Soon, I became sleepy. It seemed everything, in that chamber, was movable, removable, adjustable. Maybe flexibility is key to precision and precision makes a good surgeon. The lights, the chairs, the tables, the needles, the wires, all tools were suitable to the need of the surgeon. They adjusted my table and my head many times. The lights, the many lights above my head were blinding me and causing some discomfort.

When the first drop of blood dropped into my open mouth, I smelled a strange odor through my nose. It tasted and smelled like no other thing I knew before. I was hearing the voices of, probably, three people in the room. When my mouth got full of blood, I heard them exchange Chinese words. It was probably not the best time for me to learn Chinese. Their mouths masked of a white cloth, I could barely hear their conversation. I was asked if I was capable of comprehending in my state. I couldn't speak. They couldn't proceed. The blood was hindering every aspect of the surgery. One of them told me, in my tongue, to let the blood through. With some pain and disgust, I forced it into my stomach. This gave me room to breathe through my wounded mouth. I was almost being asphyxiated by alcohol vapors and anesthesia substances running straight into my nose. The atmosphere was becoming deletere, almost explosive. I could breathe only if I forced the blood into my stomach.

My big incisive was standing in their way, not just my blood. They probably never anticipated it.

I remember them asking my "dad" why he didn't bring me earlier, when I was a baby. They seemed a little upset. My "dad" told them about the death of my biological father. That calmed them. We lived in a remote area where police and militia payed us more visits than doctors and nurses. My body and myself were too old for a reparation surgery. The physical and psychological scars won't go away.

Now I have teeth in my mouth and more importantly, I have questions in my mind. Was I neglected to the point where they thought I wouldn't need a woman in my life?

When they started to pull out my incisive, they found it so deeply implanted, its roots so strong that all of their tools seemed inappropriate. Their sharp and small tools were dwarfed by my big and sharp incisive! They were unprepared. They resorted to improvisations. If all dentists are surgeons, all surgeons are not dentists. This Chinese and his team were not dentists. They didn't have the right tools to pull my tooth out. At first, they used a "pliers" to cut it in half.

This sent waves of pain directly into my already embroiled brain like a pebble in a boiling pond. It was becoming pure torture. These waves, from the wounded mouth and the shock from the broken tooth, were having double ripple effect into my entire body like dynamite in a building.

When they started to piece the two ends together, what was left of my tooth was still standing in the way. The operation was already taking longer than initially planned. Quickly, they decided to be radical. This leftover tooth, like a tree trunk in a soccer field, ought to be uprooted. In doing so, they took a good chunk of my gum. They even took the two hairy pieces of my broken nose. This surgical hurricane left nothing standing in its passage on my face.

I don't remember exactly when I started crying. I was deliriously calling for outside help, for divine intervention in my crusade against these barbaric surgeons. Helpless, I started to call for my mother. I was loud enough to cause disturbance into what's being done to my mouth. I believe also that people outside were alerted to my suffering, to these strange calls for help. At least, they could've been speculating about hearing voices. I was running out of everything, specially the three most precious items in a surgery: hope, air and blood. The situation became so desperate that the anesthesia dosage has to be incremented to fit these complications, these crimes against my mouth.

I may have seen them in a coma probably. But I have some recollection of a queue of people watching me being pushed away in a cart or a gurney. I was covered by a white sheet. They were watching like a coffin. They believed I was dead. My hospital bed was on the first floor. In my state, I could not have made a clear distinction between left and right, upward and downward positions. I believe, I was lifted, through the stairwell, to my room.

When I woke up, my "dad" was there, patiently awaiting a sign of life from me. His presence reassured me. Waking up from that deep sleep was a kind of resurrection. My wounded mouth was severely bandaged.

Three weeks later, I was given a mirror by my "dad" to see my mouth, my new face, my new mouth in my old face, to see my new mouth in my new face, to compare the before to the after. What happened to my old mouth? Where is my old face? My lip was still very much swollen, voluminous. I opened the bag of my mouth. Two items were missing, stolen by these unscrupulous surgeons: my precious incisive and its gum. Nothing in their place. My nose could no longer filter the dusty, filthy hospital air, city fumes and vehicle exhaust.

How can I kiss a girl with such mouth? How can I rival with my grandfather? How can I have four wives like him? when is he going to take me seriously with this new mouth? When is he going to see me as a threat to his harem? When am I going to chase him out of his territory? Mark it as my own? When am I going to send him off as he sent me off if I don't even have teeth in my mouth?

If my nose is missing essential components, how can I smell danger and adversaries like my grandfather?

How can I smell potential mates like these beautiful, perfumed, scented Fulani girls?

If I go back home, my grandfather would simply point his finger to my mouth and say I don't even have teeth to begin with, adding to my already long list of imperfections. I left with teeth, I came back like a chicken that lost its feathers in a fight. If I don't scare him with a beautiful face, he's certainly going to make my mouth more miserable than before. Thank God, I don't have any more teeth to brush in public! Would he say.

When all of the bandages fell off, I didn't have three lips anymore. But the name "Toni tati" stayed. I searched in my mind and in the sky why. I couldn't find the reason.

Under the scar, this big scar, I carried a huge psychological wound.

My grandfather is dead few years ago. But my drive, my impulse to impress him, to surpass him is still alive. All my life, I defined success as stopping my grandfather's stereotypes of me. Like in a newspaper, I wanted his caricatures of me to be more respectful of my person, specially my mouth.

For months now, my imagination is transporting me to America, probably to make it clear, once for all, that I am the strongest. I didn't want to fight local fights like my grandfather. I wanted to go and fight global fights.

My grandfather spoke only French, very little French, just enough to follow administrative orders and accommodate other encombrant guests. To make him jealous, despite my mouth and my pronunciation issues, I decided to learn English. I wanted desperately to learn English. In the entire village, there's not one single book in English. Even French is difficult to find. To distinguish himself from the illiterate, only Mody saikou had this inscription in his property: villaya. This to convey power and class.

In my grandfather's library, there's only old Islamic books. Nothing else to fight him with.

For the class of English, there's only a couple of books available. The teacher and school office thought our hands were too dirty to hold on to them. We were not even allowed to touch the pages. Often the teacher had to go around the tables to show each group of students a picture, a word, a cartoon. The books were kept out of reach. Each session, the teacher folded them minitiously, placed them in a box before putting them away. Three to four students per book. In groups, we repeated after the teacher. It sounded very foreign to us. Words and letters were written the same way as in French but pronounced very differently. How can my mouth, an operated mouth adapts to all of this? How can a mouth without proper lips, without teeth and gum pronounce all of this? How can such mouth be French in the morning and English in the afternoon?

I'm marching, like a soldier, five miles a day, to learn English, to transform my mouth into a tool to speak to the wider world unlike my grandfather who was speaking to a local audience. I was running every morning so I won't miss the English class in the afternoon because I wanted to beat my grandfather. I wanted him to hear me speak English. Even if he doesn't hear me, I wished secretly he would know that I spoke

English. I wanted to induce fear in him like in a boxing match. If my mouth spoke English, he would be afraid of making fun of it.

All year around, I run past everybody, every morning. I run past Cellou, Bakar bhoye, Bakar kowly. I run past even Moudjitaba who woke up hours earlier than I so he won't have to run. They were all wondering why. Moudjitaba, jokingly, would remark: "It's not just school you are running for, you are going beyond school today." But I didn't have time to waste in the morning when English is in noon. I didn't have time to waste if my grandfather never spoke English and I want to beat him before he starts to. I also wanted to go beyond my village after having beaten my grandfather.

If my feet were desperately running so I could learn English, my wounded mouth wasn't following.

Pronunciation was a big rock in my way to English. I was also learning philosophy. I am all excited. Philosophy and English are the best weapons against my grandfather. Armed with English and philosophy, my mouth will no longer be a handicap but an advanced weapon against my old fashioned grandfather. If he's an Imam, I am a philosoph. I am adding reason to his dogma. I am learning critical thinking. I am opening up my mind to his narrow vision of the world. If I could not change my mouth, I could change my mind, change minds and mindsets. At least, I could change my mind about my mouth. But to pronounce, you need good lips, good teeth, good gum, not just a tongue. Mines were stolen by this Chinese surgeon in a life and death fight. My teachers could tell. They could not not have known my mouth. They all could tell. My English teacher could tell. Mr. Diané, my philosophy teacher could tell. My French teacher could read it in my lips.

My biology teacher could not not have known what happened to my mouth. But they all hid it from my teasing classmates. They willingly, bravely, ignored my wounded mouth and saw the fire in me to learn. They encouraged me. They nourished my fire with their desire to serve. But they didn't know I was fighting to beat my grandfather. I wasn't just fighting to get good grades, to get ahead of my classmates. I was fighting to get even with my family, to restore my dignity after my grandfather took me for retarded. My teachers didn't know I was a wounded lion. Only my grandmother knew. She was an early witness. That's why she banged on my door, threw stones on my door to wake me up so I can go and learn English and philosophy to fight back my grandfather.

But my grandfather died before I finished my English lessons like a coward. I felt like a gladiator without a contender. What can I do to impress him in his grave? What can I accomplish to make him jealous? What can I do to make him come back and fight?

I began to think going to America will blow his mind advitam aeternam. But how America will react to my mouth?

Since my grandfather called me a cow, it's been a long way. I am looking back. In my mind, there's a mix of pictures. One was continuously coming back: my English teacher asking about the smartest student in his class and the entire high school. All of my classmates and the teacher agreed on my humble person to be that student despite my mouth. It counted for my first victory over my grandfather.

Among the hundreds of first pupils, pioneers in my village, I am the only one to compete to the end despite my mouth. The rest? They've all abandoned the race, one after the other. All of them had perfect mouths.

Mouctar? The beacon of hope for my grandfather!? He left the race as I was just beginning to wake up to our grandfather's insinuations and judgements. He too had a good mouth. Despite my mouth, the DPE has given me a prize in front of my "dad" who's attendance was demanded by the education authorities so that my family will be aware and proud of my achievement in the baccalaureate.

In yimbaya high school, I've received an unusual name in lieu et place of Toni tati: "dictionnaire vivant". There my mouth disappeared in front of my mind. Students saw what my mind was capable of, not my mouth.

More recently, despite my mouth, I've received a standing ovation in an exposé. There was talk of me being ahead of time. From being retarded to being ahead of time, the metamorphosis may have been mind blowing to anyone except my grandfather. Unless I go to America, he'll remain unconvinced in his grave.

If I am ahead of time, even Americans will accept my mouth. They might not be offended by it if and as long as I have a brain. I am thinking. I am torturing myself.

I am convincing myself it's the right thing to do. Every time I am alone, my mind can't stop wandering.

Since I am ahead of time, I'd rather be transported to the future than be dragged into the past. If I am ahead of time, I'd rather go to a civilization where the weather isn't just a daily occurrence, it is measured and predicted I'd rather have an umbrella than soak in the rain like my grandfather did in this tiny village.

If I am ahead of time, I'd rather go the civilization of Adam Smith, Keynes, Ford and Einstein than waste my time in my grandfather's village where time seems frozen, where time is lived rather than measured. In my exposé, I talked about globalization. If my brain was too small in my grandfather's eyes, the day of my exposé I felt my mind was too big to be contained in a village, to be encaged, to be chained in a closed civilization.

America became even more desirable when, by chance, I found a book. Unlike the manuals I have known, this one was rich in photographic pictures. My desire to cross the Atlantic became higher than the twin towers. The English description of these cities, monuments, attractions, was accessible to the average I was. This book was probably aimed at tourist. But the book was eaten on its edges by mice or cockroaches. I still remember the Potomac river and its description. The black and white picture of the statue of liberty was half eaten like a profanation. These illustrations gave material support to my imaginations. I can urgue with anyone about America. The book was probably also kept in a humid place or came into contact with water. Beautiful pages were glued together. How can anyone dare to neglect such a wonderful book? Does he know the weight of his ignorance? I dried it in the sun but I was still losing some of the pictures and texts turning the pages despite my delicate hands. Every time a piece peeled off, I got frustrated like losing the statue of liberty to a vandal or a terrorist. I could not stand losing these precious objects and valuable monuments to my trembling hands? I asked myself if I had Parkinson like my grandfather. If an artist or an architect could do this with his own hands, the least I could do is to turn the pages without damaging these pictures and texts.

I owed that to America and its founding fathers. The pages kept peeling off as I turned them.

My grandfather was always preaching about souls, spirits, heavens, Hellfires instead of GDP, Income, Growth or conceiving, drawing, building world computers and world towers. Why couldn't he do this? If he did this, his voice and message would've been gone higher than his altar. He would've been a world figure if he built the Brooklyn bridge instead of talking about hellfire bridges in the hereafter. His name would've been on the flatiron building or on the front pages of the New York Times. Instead of turning the old pages of a book written in the seventh century every morning after breakfast, he would've been turning the pages of the Wall Street Journal. Instead of sitting in his stoop trembling every morning, he would've been holding on the metro pole to fight his way to work. Instead of rejecting my mouth, he would've been embracing different cultures, different races, different religions. Instead of focusing on me being retarded, he would have been celebrating diversity.

To go from being a cow to a cow keeper to being a globalization expert, there was jump in time. It was a step in the moon for me. Since I am such, I'd rather go the civilization of GDP. I want to see the work of my small hands to be quantified, measured, registered, recorded. I want to hold the file of my taxes every year. I want to be on time if not ahead of time. I have to leave the civilization of my grandfather before it's too late if it is true I am ahead of time, if it is true I was the smartest of my high school.

I was hoping that they would see in my face not my mouth but my accomplishments, my intelligence. Aren't they there to detect talents? Haven't they stolen brains from all over the world? Can't they read minds?

I am thinking. I am evaluating my chances in front of an interviewing officer. What kind of qualities will he be looking for? Will he know, all of my life, I've been a fighter? Will he know that I've won against all odds? Will he know, when I was born, millions of babies were not making it to their first year? Does he know, despite my mouth, I've made it all the way to him? Does he know that I've survived my grandfather? Does he know that I don't fall to the edges of life even if I am pushed to? Will he know that I want to impress, defy and defeat my dead grandfather?

I am laying down in an old mattress on the roof of an unfinished uncle's building. It was too hot to stay indoors. My room wasn't comfortable anyway. It was humid and mushrooms were colonizing every inch of it to the edges of my broken bed. It smelled moisture. My only witness on that roof was the wide open sky. A perfect place and moment for dreaming. Words and pictures of that English book I red earlier were coming and going in my mind like the blinking stars in the sky. The American dream, like the moon in the horizon, was coming closer, brighter. The farther and wider I looked, the more stars I saw, the more dreams I got. Sangoyah where I lived didn't exist anymore. I couldn't see the buildings around me. The only skyscrapers that existed were those of my mind taken from that English book.

From time to time, I stood up to gaze, not the sky but the other wide open world: the ocean. Its vision reminded me that those who made it to the other side of the Atlantic had a plan not just a dream. A mosquito bite helped bring me to reality. I left my dreamy state to start doing business. As a globalization expert, I knew people meant business nowadays. I have to wear new clothing. I have to stop being and looking ordinary. A new costume and a new state of mind are requirements for would be successful people.

Just as I was asking myself how my mouth would fit in a costume, Alsainy silty appeared, like a ghost. I got surprised. But I have been in this building long enough for its demons to know me. I could be myself one of them. It was unusual for me to get visited there. If Alsainy, the son of my Uncle Mody Aliou silty, sought to see me in person, it has to be important, probably serious. I thought, one moment, that my grandfather has come back from the dead to give me another cow to graze in the wilderness, just to prevent me from pursuing my American dream. This time my grandmother won't be here to oppose his Machiavellian plan like when she prevented him from ruining my school education.

But his father too has died. Mody Aliou Silty has died logging trees. He fell from the top, the edge of a branch. He died instantly, hitting the hard, rocky ground head first. This is the fate my grandfather wanted me to have.

I've survived his calculated plans. No one will stop me from planning my trip to America. From the edge of a tree branch, I will go to the edge of the empire state building without falling to my grandfather's traps.

Alsainy and I sat on the edge of my old mattress. He was coming from the village. I was anxious. In just three years, I've lost my grandfather and my grandmother. Both died in my absence. My step dad has become the new Imam after a long battle with half of the village that wasn't supportive, aborting a coup d'etat against him plotted by Alhadji babagalle who hired killers to go after him, took a machete to decapitate him at that altar of the mosque. This was equivalent to a nation going through a revolution inside of my family. My village and my people were in turmoil. I still remember my "dad" and Alhadji Babagalle compete for audiences, each one claiming to be on a mission to revive the Islamic tradition under constant attack by the misguided, the unguided and the imported western decadence. Alcohol, dancing, women, women clothing and fashion were their favorite topics. They were both in favor of sharia implementation and enforcement. But there was only one seat. They were both preparing to take my grandfather's seat. Well before his death, each camp was sharpening its arsenal. The mosque was to be a theatre where dust was to fly and blood to be spilled. I was anxious because of this volatile situation:

"I am here to inform you, on your mother's behalf, that your "dad" has come to ask her for divorce. She said she had no choice but to accept." Said Alsainy.

After a long sigh, I find myself obligated to ask:

"Why?"

"No apparent reason. She said she heard rumors. She said he said he wanted an amicable separation. She'll keep all of her rights except she'll no longer share his bed."

I was embarrassed to hear that but I have to continue this conversation:

"Did my mother commit a crime?"

"No."

"Did she commit a grave mistake?"

"No."

I wanted to ask if she cheated on him but I didn't know how to handle such heavy word.

My mouth was still open and my mind searching the right wording when Alsainy added:

"According to rumors, he wants to marry again."

"Again?" I asked loudly and vehemently like I wanted my dad to hear my exasperation and my opposition. I continued.

"How many does one need? He has already Nan Ismaila, my own mother, Nan Kadiatou pellel, Nan Diamilatou bournoumou.

"He's allowed only four wives. To marry again, one of the four has to die or divorce."

"Couldn't he wait until my mother's death?"

Why does he have to marry again?

Alsainy left. I have now more questions than answers. Why my mother? She wasn't the ugliest. She was even prettier. Once she told me she was miss of the revolutionary communist regime. She wasn't rebellious. In fact, she was the most submissive of them in part because of her vulnerability as a former widow. Her cuisine and toilet were the best. She was elegant in her fashion. She wore her smile on all occasions. Her smile and laughter were even contagious. She treated guests and unannounced visitors equally well.

What went through my dad's head? Was he so much in love that he lost his mind? Did he feel above and beyond because of his coronation as imam? Does he feel like the strong man after my grandfather's death? What my grandmother was thinking of him in her grave? Sure he would have never dared such thing in her lifetime. She would have never approved. It was clearly an offense to anyone who knew my mother. The dignity and honor of the family were in jeopardy. If he wanted to add standing to his persona, he has certainly missed his goal. Probably he did this for lust. He wasn't beautiful as a young man. He used to have rotten teeth which wasn't too attractive to beautiful young ladies. Probably, he wanted to satisfy past desires, catch up with his youth.

Like the clouds in the sky, my thoughts were darkening under the heavy weight of this news. Like my mother, I felt depreciated, undervalued, betrayed.

How can an Imam throw the holy books at my mother? How can he talk about wrongs and decadences in the mosque and do this at home? How can he warn the strong against the weak and use his position of power to his advantage? How can I call him dad again?

For a long time, I believed he was my real dad until my grandmother told me my story, the story of the day she had to bury her son and cradle her grandson. A herse in one hand and a cradle in the other. The story of the day she had to dig a grave and extract me out of the belly of my mother. She told people it looked like I came out of that grave to replace her son (did my lip get cut in two pieces during that process?). It was the day mourners came to celebrate life, the confusing day where people didn't know if they should cry or smile. But how can anyone smile in front of a baby with such disfigured face? Was it really two tragedies for my family, specially my mother and my grandmother? Did my mouth cause my biological dad to die the day I was born? Or Did his death cause my mother to deliver me? My grandmother didn't want me to be dadless. So she "fabricated" a new dad for me. Despite Mouctar's protestations, his dad became my dad. My uncle Addouramani inherited us: my mother, my older sister and I. His first wife was Nan Ismaila, of dark complexion like coal. She was a descendant of former slaves on one side. Mouctar, of my age, my grandfather's beacon of hope, was their first born child.

His third wife was Nan Kadiatou pellel. She was light skinned and beautiful. But she had rotten front teeth like he used to. She was perfect until she smiled.

His fourth wife was Nan Diamilatou. She was quite "old" when he got married to her. In my village, if girls are pretty, they got married earlier, sooner, younger. She accepted him because of her "age." All of her friends have tied the knot already.

So all of the conquest of my uncle Addouramani were women in vulnerable situations, women with insecurities.

Now that he's in a dominant position, he's been crowned king of the mosque, he gets to choose the woman of his taste, he gets to select the females of his harem. From being an unsecured man, he's become the Alfa male, the new "holy" star. Like a politician's make over in a looming election, he replaced his bad teeth with good ones when he felt his father's general health was declining, deteriorating. An imam with rotten teeth won't have good following. His message would be lost in his teeth. They'll cause the congregation to be distracted, his authority to be diminished.

This divorce conversation separated me from my American dream just for the time being. Its ghost came back as soon as Alsainy's physical presence disappeared in the dark stairs of the one story building. It came back more intense than before. If I was looking for the right reasons to go to America, now I've found a lite motive. Like dogma to religions, this unilateral divorce added to the many dogmatic forces that were attracting me to America. If I were in America, probably my "dad" would've thought twice before picking on us. If I were in America, my mother would not have been vulnerable. If I were in America, I would've been making decisions about our family's life and death, not my "dad". If I were in America, he would not have dared to attack my mother in my absence.

I was marching, wandering all over the roof. I leaned on the edges many times like a distraught suicidal. But if I commit suicide, I won't go to America nor to paradise. One moment, I realized I was facing Fatim's home. I immediately began thinking of her, remembering her last words to me.

A few days ago, I overcame my fear of girls and told Fatim that I was in love with her. For four years, I've been waiting for an opportunity. If you have my mouth, girls don't give you opportunities. For four years I've been watching her. Fatim was gracious. My favorite moment to watch her was when she was doing laundry in their yard. I've never set foot there nor inside of their mushroomed house. But from outside I could see their old, broken furniture. Windows and doors were almost inexistent. It seemed they moved in too early or too late. The aspect of the house, its furniture, every little broken thing they had made Fatim even more attractive to me. Her beauty contrasted with every ugly item they possessed. Their simplicity seemed neglect. Her sparkling dark skin resembled the charcoal they sold to make a living. When she was washing and drying in the sun, she made herself look like a girl in a beach. She would wear a short pink towel and a bra. She used to have a white towel too. But one day, she stopped wearing it. When washing her bra, she'd adjust her towel just above her breasts, enough to conceal, just short of revealing. Her towel was too short to not betray her beautiful, firm legs. Fatim was the girl next door. I used my one story building as a watching tower. I managed to watch her through the leafy orange and mango branches. I would go as far as to cut or rearrange them to see her better. I watched her through every window and hole of the building.

For four years, Fatim's graciousness remotely controlled my attention. I'm sure, I got her attention too. She could not have not seen my mouth. She may have seen it daily. To go anywhere, I had to pass by their house. Our home was a dead end. An SOS village was built in the middle of the street corner. For four years, I expected her to invite me one-day in. But when you have my mouth, girls never invite you home. She rejected my offer immediately arguing that she had a boyfriend. It was in front of Keita who has purported to help. Keita was very successful, very talented with girls. He'd asked me many times why I didn't have a girl. One day, I told him about Fatim. In one short evening, he accomplished what I couldn't accomplish in four years. He approached Fatim naturally, held her hand like a true gentleman and asked her to come with him like an old friend for a short walk. Before I woke up to his daring dating, he's finished telling her about me and my feeling towards her. Not him nor her mentioned my mouth. But my mouth was present in all our three heads. How could I be successful in love? My thoughts about America came to the surface again. If I were in America, Fatim would've never rejected me. If I were in America, Fatim would've rolled her eyes in admiration of me, my style, my fashion, my swag. She would've wagged her tail for me. If I were in America, she would've kissed my lip, my entire mouth. If I were in America, Fatim would've been all over me. If I were in America, I would not have wasted four years of my life (time for a master's degree) to get a girl. If I were an American, I would've acted boldly, swiftly like a GI. If I were in America, Fatim would've waited for me for four years, for forty years if I were American. If I were in America, Fatim would've watched me through their broken windows, through every opening, through every hole of their old, mushroomed house.

"Give me your name" Mody Aliou Tougue asked me.

"Mamadaibou." I said.

"I need your full name." He insisted.

I wasn't used to giving my other name. Seeing my confusion, he came to the rescue:

"Bah, Barry, Diallo, sow...?"

"Diallo." I replied.

He wrote my name on a piece of paper.

"What's your mother's name?"

"Hassanatou."

"Her full name, please. I need that for your American dream to come true." He said boldly.

I don't know what led me there. But when I told Mody Aliou Tougue about my American project, when he insisted he he is the perfect man for the job, I started to believe it couldn't be just chance. It was a divine intervention. His room felt like my grandfather's. It was simply furnished with some visible but innocent disorganization. As to have them handy, he was surrounded with pages of tricky figures, numbers, graphics in Arabic. In a corner, burning encens filled the room with discreet smoke of good smell:

"Diallo." I said about my mother's name, adding:

"But my uncle is standing in my way to America. He doesn't wanna spent his money on such dream." Anyone opposed to my going to America was automatically classified as an enemy and placed in the axe of evil. I was ready for war.

"Give me his full name as well." Mody Aliou Tougue demanded in a strong and loud voice. His wife who was bathing her baby and cooking outside could guess what my visit was about now.

For a moment, I thought he was going to grant me a visa. He had such confidence that I, myself, started to believe in my chances. When he told about his past performances, his predictions about past weathers, past political outcomes, I couldn't wait to see the weather and the politics going on in the American embassy. What weather, what politics will I get? "For anything to happen, for any prayer to be granted, the earth and the sky need to be perfectly aligned. I'll ask the sovereign of the earth and the sky this night of Thursday to Friday to align them for your American dream to come true. I'll enter khalwa tonight."

Khalwa is this spiritual, mystic exercise, it: is this journey in which the spirits will tell if I was going to make it to America. When appropriately done, all procedures, protocols followed, they'll come from the hidden world and reveal to him the unknown.

When I came out of his dark chamber, I lifted my head to the blue sky as to fly to the skyscrapers I admired months earlier in that old book. I felt wings growing in me. The only time I felt so good about myself was in my teacher's classrooms. Like them, Mody Aliou Tougue gave me confidence in myself.

Like in my teacher's classrooms, I forgot my difference in his presence. He made me forget my mouth. He was so engaging that he brought to my memory my first teacher, Mouse Ousmane and the very first time he asked the classroom to write "Monsieur" on our small boards.

Everyone got flogged for their incorrect spelling except me, Toni tati. It was our first year of French. It was a sign the communist regime was dead. When it came to power, French was abolished and national languages reinstated in the curriculum. That spelling day constituted the beginning of my "intellectual revolution". The praise I got from Mouse Ousmane made me feel like the first steel of the industrial revolution. It made me feel stronger, unbeatable.

I felt some closeness to him. He seemed capable of easing the pains of my soul. I felt the need to tell him not just my name but the story behind my name, the story of my mouth. wanted not just to tell him my mother's full name but her ordeal as well. I wanted to tell him about Fatim and all of my frustrations about love. Mody Aliou Tougue, unlike my grandfather, seemed to know me from the day I was born when I fell from the back of my mother and didn't even cry. He seemed to be there that day and saw my strength and my resolve to fight and keep on going despite my mouth and my grandfather. He told me a bright future was ahead of me. Everything wasn't gloom and doom, deficiencies and malformations unlike my grandfather's forecasting of my destiny.

On the eve of my interview appointment at the embassy, he managed to put America in a padlock. When he passed it to me, I could still feel the energy he put in it. I also felt the warmth of his magnetic arms. He told me:

"Lock it and go!"

The earth and the sky were perfectly aligned. In a table of numbers, 3 and 4 appeared in order. In Arabic, they looked like African sculptures. "The 3 is for the sky, the 4 is for the earth", he explained. The pursuit of happiness will not just be a word in the constitution. It will be pronounced and spelled by Toni tati's limping mouth.

In the early morning of my interview, seated on the benches of the embassy, I was hoping and praying that a lip more or a lip less won't disqualify me for the spelling competition. H-A-P-P-I-N-E-S-S pursuit was all my mouth wished not to mispronounce or misspell.

My limping mouth will probably fall. But it will not cry since I fell from the back of my mother and didn't even cry. From an orange tree, my grandfather expected my mouth to fall to the ground breaking it in even more pieces. From the edge of a cliff, he lured it to its death without any success, intending to blame it on ADD. Probably it'll have the last word. To my grandfather's demise, my lip did more than just eating, it spoke English. It'll probably make that giant leap to America as well.

I America, I may stumble and fall because of my limping mouth. But I'll not cry.

When I fell from the back of my mother, I didn't have teeth to lose then. I just didn't want my grandfather to see me cry therefore take me for granted. Now that I 've lost my teeth in a fight with a Chinese surgeon, I don't want my grandfather to see the hole in my mouth if ever I cried in America.

www.ingramcontent.com/pod-product-compliance
Lightning Source LLC
Chambersburg PA
CBHW030104100526
44591CB00008B/261